Children

by Jennifer L. Marks

Consulting Editor: Gail Saunders-Smith, PhD

Capstone
press®

Mankato, Minnesota

Pebble Books are published by Capstone Press,
151 Good Counsel Drive, P.O. Box 669, Mankato, Minnesota 56002.
www.capstonepub.com

Library of Congress Cataloging-in-Publication Data
Marks, Jennifer, 1979–
    Children / by Jennifer L. Marks. — Rev. and updated ed.
    p. cm. — (Pebble books. People)
    Includes bibliographical references and index.
    Summary: "In simple text and photos, presents children and what they do" — Provided by publisher.
    ISBN-13: 978-1-4296-2237-0 (hardcover)
    ISBN-10: 1-4296-2237-7 (hardcover)
    ISBN-13: 978-1-4296-3460-1 (softcover)
    ISBN-10: 1-4296-3460-X (softcover)
    1. Children — Juvenile literature. I. Title. II. Series.
HQ781.M29 2009
305.231 — dc22   2008026506

Note to Parents and Teachers

The People set supports national social studies standards related to individual development and identity. This book describes and illustrates children. The images support early readers in understanding the text. The repetition of words and phrases helps early readers learn new words. This book also introduces early readers to subject-specific vocabulary words, which are defined in the Glossary section. Early readers may need assistance to read some words and to use the Table of Contents, Glossary, Read More, Internet Sites, and Index sections of the book.

Printed in the United States of America in Stevens Point, Wisconsin.
042011   006165

Table of Contents

All about Children

Children are busy,
growing people.
Children grow up
to become adults.

Parents love
and take care
of their children.

8

What Children Do

Children grow.

Megan grew
taller last year.

Children learn.

Grace reads about horses.

Children play.

Eddie goes

to baseball practice.

Helping

Children do chores.

Nate takes out
the garbage.

Lisa sets the table
for dinner.

Bob and his brother
rake leaves into a pile.

Children are important family members.

Glossary

adult — a person who is fully grown

chore — a job that has to be done regularly, such as washing dishes or cleaning

dinner — the main meal of the day

family — a group of people related to one another

parent — a mother or a father of one child or many children

rake — to use a garden tool with metal teeth to collect leaves, grass cuttings, and other things

Read More

Easterling, Lisa. *Families.* Our Global Community. Chicago: Heinemann, 2007.

Kelley, Michelle. *Just Like You.* My Day at School. Vero Beach, Fla.: Rourke, 2007.

Internet Sites

FactHound offers a safe, fun way to find educator-approved Internet sites related to this book.

Here's what you do:
1. Visit *www.facthound.com*
2. Choose your grade level.
3. Begin your search.

This book's ID number is 9781429622370.

FactHound will fetch the best sites for you!

Index

Word Count: 67
Grade: 1
Early-Intervention Level: 12

Credits
Sarah L. Schuette, editor; Abbey Fitzgerald, designer; Marcy Morin, photo
   shoot scheduler

Photo Credits
Capstone Press/Karon Dubke, all

The author dedicates this book to Pops and his three goats.